Stewart Henderson was born in Liverpool in 1952, and since his teens has been performing his poetry on radio, television and stage. He has appeared on numerous occasions on BBC Radio's 1, 2, 3, 4 and 5 Live, the World Service, and BBC TV, RTE, ITV as well as various US and European national channels. He has read his work at many major venues throughout the UK, Republic of Ireland, USA and Canada, including London's Royal Albert Hall, Glasgow's SECC, Dublin's National Concert Hall, Belfast's Ulster Hall, Cardiff's St David's Hall, and New York's Lincoln Center for Performing Arts.

Stewart's poems now appear in many anthologies and text books. His first collection of verse for children *Who Left Grandad at the Chip Shop?* published by Lion Books, quickly became a best-seller when it appeared in the late summer of 2000. He is also known as a writer and presenter of feature documentaries for BBC Radio.

By the same author

Poetry:

CARVED INTO A SCAN
WHOSE IDEA OF FUN IS A NIGHTMARE?
FAN MALE
ASSEMBLED IN BRITAIN
A GIANT'S SCRAPBOOK
HOMELAND
LIMITED EDITION

Poetry for Children:

WHO LEFT GRANDAD AT THE CHIP SHOP?

General:

GREENBELT: SINCE THE BEGINNING
ADRIFT IN THE 80S: THE STRAIT INTERVIEWS
(Editor)

This could only ever be for
my beloved Carol

unwavering and unchanging
and with all that
tender and supportive love

ACKNOWLEDGEMENTS

All Things Pass; God Of . .; Inspiration; Where Does God Come From?; and *All Things New* were commissioned by BBCTV for use in various programmes. *The Mamod Little Dynamo; Underneath the Arches; Masterchef; Kit Inspection;* and *Sitting Comfortably* were commissioned by BBC Radio 4 for the series *In Celebration* - my thanks especially to David Prest for bringing these poems into being. *Holy City* was written for a special performance in Liverpool's Anglican Cathedral. *Thunder and Rainbows* is also in song form with music by Martyn Joseph (Pipe Records/Waif Music). In the final section of this volume are some poems from my earlier books, now out of print, for which I receive frequent requests.

I am particularly grateful to J.John for commissioning *The Ten of Hearts* sequence of poems - and for his belief in me. Other poems were written for various public readings - my thanks to all those who organised these events. I am especially indebted to Eddie, Mary Jane and Abigail Donaldson for such wholesome support and friendship, and in a similar vein also my huge thanks to John and Sarah Webb; Simon and Alison Dennis; Bill Manners; Glenys Buckingham; David and Heather Tucker; and all our dear fellow 'High-Wirers'.

Still, facing Autumn would not have happened, (been edited, typeset, designed and appeared) had it not been for the love, skill, patience and determination of Carol, my wife, my mate and my unique love. Her courage through adversity is a true fact and an inspiration.

TABLE OF CONTENTS

Still, facing Autumn	1
God of . . .	2
Anxious	3
Holy City	5
Me and all my friends	8
Outstanding natural beauty	10
Easter in February	12
Talking to Jupiter	13
Arisaig House	14
All my . .	16
On reflection	17
Drawing	18
Where did God come from?	19
Stags on the foreshore	20
Inspiration	26
Best wishes for the season	27
Thunder and Rainbows	28
Seasonal Sonnet 2: Summer	30
Seasonal Sonnet 4: Winter	31
Lunar tourist	32
Housing Benefits	34
Straw hat dreams	35
Gone away for a while	36
Cenotaph	38
Eating with God	39
Family stories	40
Chase	41
All things new	42

Song of the worm	44
All things pass	46
Sometimes love	47
Of all roses	48

IN CELEBRATION

Kenwood capers	50
The Mamod Little Dynamo	52
Sitting comfortably	53
Underneath the arches	54
Kit Inspection	56

TEN OF HEARTS

No. 1	59
No. 2	61
No. 3	62
No. 4	64
No. 5	66
No. 6	67
No. 7	69
No. 8	71
No. 9	73
No.10	74

COMMON PRAYERS

How to build a sanctuary	76
God beyond gold	77
Grieving	78
Here's hoping	79
London Marathon	80

BY SPECIAL REQUEST

I believe	82
I'm dousing myself	87
Word Perfect	88
Hip op rappity rap	90
This day in Paradise	92

Still, facing Autumn

In the fire and frailty
of this gathering season
let us rake up
our accumulated months.

It will be a collection of
haunting curios and
uneven treasures,
permanent chronicles
and ashen memories.
So let the looted, spoiled days burn
they cannot char the golden urn.

In the shaping and stacking
of this pruning season,
when there are a few, final flowers
let us be
still, facing Autumn
as the soil turns over
and becomes amethyst
whilst sleeping,
and the wombs of muted roots
brood with honey and hue.

For what appears as in demise
then contradicts,
what's dead can rise.

GOD OF . . .

God of the molecule
God of the pearl
God of the calorie-filled
Coconut Whirl

God of the wayward
God of the saints
God of the broken-faced
bouncers' restraints

God of mid-winter
God of the bleaker
God of the hounded
asylum seeker

God of engagement-ringed
pretty bank tellers
God of evicted
Big Issue sellers

God of the addict
coming off stuff
God of the desert
God of enough

ANXIOUS

I'm anxious when I'm working
I'm anxious if I'm not,
the emotional equivalent
of flying Aeroflot.

I'm anxious when I'm thinking
I'm anxious when I speak,
I'm an Eiger of uncertainty,
a self-esteemless peak.

I'm anxious about insects
so I'm anxious in a tent,
I'm global warming twitchy now,
with scorpions in Kent.

I'm anxious of tornadoes
their annihilating might,
I'm anxious of the winged-kind
which drop cluster bombs at night.

I'm anxious about skin-tone
I'm anxious I'm not taller,
I'm anxious that the truth is
slowly getting smaller.

I'm anxious that I'm temporary
a slaughterhouse-bound sheep,
and any depth I have is like
my tattoo - just skin deep.

I'm anxious about stomach pains
and the surgeon's knife,
will I end up in a docu-soap
about the afterlife?

I'm anxious how anxiety
insidiously grew,
but most of all I'm anxious how
it's stopped me seeing you.

HOLY CITY
*[commissioned for an Urban
Conference in Liverpool]*

How holy sits this city
blessed with people.
We, the offspring of funeral famine
and market forces slavery.
We, the grandchildren
of now closed chapels
and sandstone suburbs.
Here in this city of resignation
and - 'over the water' - aspiration.

How lonely sits this city
bruised with people.
In England, but not of it.
Feeling ourselves punished
and shamed,
talking to the world through
soap operas, drag queens,
and website footballers.

City in deep mourning.
Looking back, sore with nostalgia
to our First Communion
when we were dressed pure,
and knew nothing but that moment
of absolution and acceptance -

The Body of Christ
The Blood of Christ
- and a ham tea afterwards.
How anxious sits this city
stubbed with people.
Smoking our evenings
through pub-quiz nights.
Swaggering home in the dark,
having had a few.
Remembering our childhood,
and those glossy coloured
plastic windmill thingys
on a stick
you could buy at West Kirby.
Sentimental city,
not right with itself.

How holy sits this city
blessed with people
Nowhere near paradise
but not far from it.
On probation. On drugs.
Honor Blackman
- with a joke for every occasion,
a quip at most unsuitable times.
Unruly, but helpful,
like broadcasting
The Laughing Policeman

in a mortuary
to cheer everyone up.
City of philosophers
lacking any formal training.

Surrealists without a paintbrush
knowing there are too many
gaps in the world;
as we pray before the bleak altar:
'Christ,
flayed raw to pay our toll,
have You ointment for our soul?'

And though even now,
as happy powder changes hands
not far from here,
yet still . . .

. . .How holy sits this city,
blessed with people.

ME AND ALL MY FRIENDS

I can't go in the garden
and I daren't go up the stair
I'm being scrutinised and filmed
by happy people everywhere
who are sanding, painting, potting
and annihilating drab
meanwhile Carol Smillie's hugging me
and saying 'it looks fab'.

Davina is discussing me
with Airport's Jeremy
and Laurence Llewelyn-Bowen
has feng-shuied my lavatory
though we had a lacy tiff,
Laurence said I'd stripped his soul
when I put the knitted poodle back
on my spare toilet roll.

In my lime and gingham kitchen
dear Rolf Harris smiles and blubs
whilst he's selotaping magpie's wings
and feeding them on grubs
some of which he's passed to Jamie
as The Naked Chef then takes
and grates them in his mixing bowl
for 'pukka Eccles Cakes'.

When all this business started
I could not decide what's true
so I 'phoned the police for help
but they came with a camera crew.
Then the Sarge went into make-up
now there's auburn in his hair,
he's a dame this year in panto
alongside Lionel Blair.

Charlie Dimmock's bashed my ankle
with a slab of best York stone.
Gaby Roslin's checked the x-ray,
it's a fracture of the bone -
and this being television
it takes half an hour to heal,
now I'm chased by panting cameras
and asked 'How do you feel?'

Is there no way to avoid
this crazed fiesta of the cursed,
this chirpy Hades of the lens
where natural is rehearsed?
I crave peace and isolation
from this permanent dismay,
so I've found this hermit's cave
- on a place called Taransay.

OUTSTANDING NATURAL BEAUTY

As I have approximately
two hundred acres
of blood cells in my body
I have recently declared myself
a small estate
and will be applying for
agricultural subsidies
to develop myself further.

I have plans to turn
my heart into
something spectacular
involving freesias
and scented meadows;
whilst my liver
will be landscaped
and become a walled garden
with herbaceous borders.
I will also be replacing
my ear-drums with ravens
so I can hear myself fly.
In time I will become
an exotic aviary
whilst the dense forests
of my intestines
support rare breeds of monkeys.

As I get older
and the maintenance of the estate
becomes costly
I will be charging
all medical personnel,
especially those wearing surgical gloves,
a substantial entrance fee
to stroll through my grounds
or enter my fascinating caves,
and should any of them
be so uncivilised
as to litter my cultivated insides
with their implements, syringes
and un-dissolved stitches,
they will incur substantial fines
which will go towards
the funding of a donkey sanctuary
I'll be building in my spleen.

After all, this estate is unique,
invaluable, and commands
spectacular views of my soul
although, like Utopia,
this final treasure can only be seen
from a phosphorous distance.
And as it has a preservation order on it,
under no circumstances should it be
excavated for transient research
purposes.

EASTER IN FEBRUARY

Dog looks at cat,
a blithe afternoon
both nodding off
in a sun sprawling room.

Chin lists on paw,
and haunches splayed loose,
narcissi outside
declaring Spring's truce.

Talking to Jupiter

On a billowing Kenyan plain
a matriarch elephant
gathers and counts her nursery
of unwary, larking babies.

Hoisting her telescope trunk
she scans and sniffs
the spatial, grass ocean
for the portent of
circling lions
and claw-trimmed men
with telescopic blow pipes.

Once, on a night of particular grief
and small corpses,
she raged at the
biggest planet visible
and howled hymns of unbelief.

Now, she no longer speaks to Jupiter,
her memory is gouged,
and she cannot remember
what it was like
not to be hunted by disappointment.

ARISAIG HOUSE

[*Arisaig House, a large secluded country house (now a hotel) set in beautiful, manicured grounds in the Western Highlands of Scotland, was the training location during W.W.II for the clandestine and subversive Special Operations Executive. Active behind enemy lines, some of the men and women of SOE were subsequently captured, interrogated, sent to concentration camps and executed.*]

Between the ticking of the clock
and the rustle of the rose
where swallows steep
the sloping skies
a different garden grows.

No ivy crawls or corkscrews there
around the thornless gorse,
the harebell glades
are only reached
by rueful paths of morse.

And some came to this verdant shade,
these lawns of liberty,
via Dachau, barn,
and holding cell,
and copse of treachery.

Where is this veil,
this unlike bliss,
this far felicity?
It is the place they drink the stars,
the last tranquillity.

Between the ticking of the clock
and the rustle of the rose
where spirits are
sewn back to life,
the final garden grows.

ALL MY...

all my songs are timid
and all my steps are small
You skip prism oceans
and swab the cattle stall

all my strength is fissile
and all my play lacks glee
You spin jokes with atoms,
and skittish chemistry

all my tasks are twilight
and all my efforts dusk
You yield ancient riddles
and hide the mammoth's tusk

all my breaths are driftwood
and all my blood impure
You left perfect fluid
on earth's vindictive shore

and all my seesaw yearnings
and all my famished trust
are fed in Your last banquet
of wine and wounded crust.

On Reflection

On reflection, who are we?
A disparate community,
successful and suppliant
and chemically reliant,
amassing PEPs, and deep in hock,
we are Your awaiting flock.

On reflection, where are we?
Off course in open territory,
astrologers through astral sums
confetti us with arid crumbs;
we seek the Star, so do not mock,
we are Your awaiting flock.

On reflection, what are we?
Paupers of prosperity;
the village trimmed,
the council crammed,
the aspirant,
and the socially damned,
in Barrett close and tower block,
we are Your awaiting flock.

So on reflection, will you be
portraitures of charity
excavating tenderly the wreckage
where our souls should be?
We waste on sand, but crave the Rock -
for we are Your awaiting flock.

DRAWING

Within her reams of dreams
from Babel towers of sleep,
a dowry of perplexing keys
the past has made her keep.

Within her reams of dreams
a coarse, subconscious din.
These reams of dreams
which obfuscate
by being
paper thin.

WHERE DID GOD COME FROM?

What was before God?
And from where did God come
before God arrived?
And, furthermore,
what does God remember about it?

How big is God's memory?
Bigger than China?
Or, like bone china,
which when you hold it to the light
all you see is more light
but denser light?

Is God like us?
But needing
a cosmic mantelpiece
full of silver-framed recollections
of planets that He's made?
Or are we God's memory?
Full of journeys and reminiscences
a reminder that we were before,
are, and will be?

STAGS ON THE FORESHORE
[on Scotland's devolution]

For years now
you have stalked and studied us,
dragged us through the turning bracken
at the day's deep end,
mixed our likeness
with palette knives,
and pinned us to canvas,
thinking you have captured us.

You have decapitated us,
our heads becoming
shooting party ornaments
for The Big House;
our torso hanging in the larder -
you waiting for the correct time
to slice off our richness,
our flanks full
of herb and sorrel
made fleshly firm by our once trotting
and leaping freedom.
How systematic you have been with us.

And after the trigger pounced,
you wrote books
about how noble we were,
how inscrutable we were,
how subservient we were,

neglecting to mention
how missing we were
as you filled the glens
with your emptiness
and with the graves
of crumbling crofts -
a conquest of space and solitude
where there once was us.

Yet on this August evening,
we are standing once more
on our own still, stone beach,
radiant in the burning beam
of the searchlight sun.
There is just us,
and, of course, the midge -
our very own wee, acid one-liner
which apparently we're quite
famous for,
acid one-liners that is.
You say that when we speak them
you cannot always understand us.
That has been one of your criticisms of us.
Which is weird, really, because
we can understand you -
well, the words you say anyway.
And as for your complaints about
our tongue - why not look upon it
as a role reversal which we undertook -
we, the servants, speaking French

in order to conceal our hearts
from you.

So please forgive what you may detect as
chippiness and measured joy.
It's just us getting used
to not being shot at.
And because of the imposition
of strained equality that now exists
between us,
we will have to re-negotiate our feelings.
But let us not become
bitter or hostile,
for that will be the end of us both.
We will need to forgive you your sins
and, in so doing, we will grow.

And as we are moving on
to more equal ground,
could we suggest a few points
for future discussion?

We do not wish to be pedantic,
or miserable,
but when you return to
East Sussex, Orpington and Norfolk
(your own lands)
could you possibly refrain,
when chatting with your friends,
from describing The Cuillins,
The Sound of Mull, and The Great Glen,

as 'nice', and 'lovely', and 'picturesque'.
Why not describe them as 'the shrouded
breasts of scree on which you dreamed',
or, 'the torrents grazing', or even,
'God playing'?
Or, better still,
be dumb, and become wise
before such sculptures.

So, if possible,
no more clichés to describe us.
After all, what is a cliché,
at the end of the day?
Yes, that was another one-liner,
we can't help it.
It was our way of keeping
the firing squad amused.

And, whilst we're on the subject,
we would like to discuss
your recent prejudices regarding us.
Could you please stop
imagining us as inhabiting
a leaking, mildewed manse
in which Andy Stewart, Molly Weir,
the Krankies,
Scottie dog 'fridge magnets,
taciturn Highlanders,
and Irvine Welsh,
taking tea and drugs
together with bridal slices,

dry as tumbleweed oat cakes,
and clootie dumpling,
accompanied by scratch accordion music
with drunk men in the corner
considering thistles - the whole evening
ending with the epilogue, and the police.

Oh, how can we make you understand us
with our several tongues:
'Gis a break'
'Che dol'
'There's you'
'Whaddyer mean, yer closin' the bar?'
Yes, you're right - that was another
one-liner,
and a cliché
and self-inflicted.
See how damaged we have become?

How can we make you understand
our nuances
our silences
our unsaid grief
our desire for reason
and good conclusions,
our bigotries, and blessings,
our, at times,
rasping opinions about God -
the God you appear to be phasing out
on your way to becoming civilised
and desolate.

Yes, I know that some of us still
march about God
and, as we do, He disappears.
We think He may be away
to comfort the one
who's still wailing
over the venom in us all.

So, here we are,
on the foreshore on a sublime evening
with Ben Cruachan vivid
and, seemingly, rising,
like we both could, as our antlers,
once your trophies,
become again what they once were -
the framework for wings,
now advantageously placed
because wings always crave
the better view
constantly excited at their
impending journey;
they are only waiting
for the tissue and skin to grow.

Following that, we will be
attempting resurrection
from our bullied past.

And, when we rise,
we would like to say to you:
'Will you join us?'

INSPIRATION

From where does inspiration come?
The braking bus, the grandeur slum
Graffiti rants on passive walls,
from students on their way to halls.

The sideways drunk,
whose legs won't work,
the tummy bulge of Captain Kirk,
the rhododendron's scarlet blaze,
malignant words time can't erase.

The honeyed smoke of burning peat,
the prayer-still Sunday morning street.
From where does inspiration come?
The weathered days of everyone.

Best Wishes for the Season

funny place
sickly smells
and not much sign
of jingle bells

funny presents
donkeys bray -
frankincense
soon burns away,

though gold's quite good
but myrrh is weird -
that's what you give
the disappeared

rather sparse
festivity
no needle shedding
Christmas tree

funny do
no merry tunes
no crackers, carols
or balloons

no Christmas cake
with marzipan
when God became
an also-ran.

THUNDER AND RAINBOWS

The light or the shade
concealed or displayed
enemies, friends
opposite ends

Bitter or sweet
ruffled or neat
feathers or lead
silent or said

Generous or mean
corporate or green
vagrant or lord
the dove or the sword

Distinct or obscure
prosperous or poor
devil or saint
we are and we ain't

> *Intricate mysteries*
> *life's secret codes*
> *Cul-de-sac signposts*
> *on yellow brick roads*
> *Ambiguous answers -*
> *the question's still: 'Why?'*
> *Thunder and rainbows*
> *from the same sky*

Champagne or dust
banquet or crust
authentic or fake
angel or snake

Flower or thorn
pristine or torn
desert or sea
the throne and the tree

> *Intricate mysteries*
> *life's secret codes*
> *Cul-de-sac signposts*
> *on yellow brick roads*
> *Ambiguous answers -*
> *the question's still: 'Why?'*
> *Thunder and rainbows*
> *from the same sky*

SEASONAL SONNET 2: SUMMER
by Catherine Ode

Hark! here we are in summer's grasp -
the hover-mower's harassed rasp!
And other wounds berate our ears -
pink-shouldered loons on flaking piers
loud belching out their lager songs -
too bully beef to wear sarongs!
Their lassies wedged in bargain shorts
with buggy babes burnt out of sorts
whose crimson wails now pierce their hol
for 'Carl forgot the parasol'!
Whilst ice-cream vans shrill serenade
both scorching streets and esplanade
So, hark! the blazing bougainvillaea -
for summer's here, and
the birds sound trillier!

SEASONAL SONNET 4: WINTER
by Catherine Ode

Hark! shiver hard these muted fields
where crows caw-caw
and nothing yields
as winter smothers agriculture
a suffocating, spread-winged vulture!
Though whiskered carol singers' dins
and Rotary Club collecting tins
clink and chorus Yuletide thoughts
yet young shoplifters doth get caught!
For winter paupers everyone
by creeping moods and lack of sun,
whilst dormice dare not go outdoors
a Yeti, high up, trails its spoors!
Hark! here we are in winter's web
with burst-pipe frosts until next Feb!

LUNAR TOURIST

I'm going to be a cosmic yobbo
I'm going to be a lunar louse
create tabloid shame
shouting racist names
in a Klingon curry house

I'm going to be a space-flight rowdy
and cause terrestrial distress
going to goad and bait
and humiliate
some Venusian stewardess

I'm going to brawl and ruck
with Triffids
I'm going to crush a Dalek flat
and make history as I pulp ET
with a temporal baseball bat

I'm going to build a solar theme pub
and ban Martians from the bar
put on meteor swarms
where the beer is warm
the first segregated star

And when there I'll get all sentimental
recalling what made home so great
St. Ives, St. George, and Cheddar Gorge
lemon curd and chauvinistic hate

I'm going to take this tribal message
from the planet of my birth
for I'm a pit-bull,
an astral John Bull,
I'm a patriot of Earth.

Housing Benefits

snowmen don't go for a sauna
ducks never bother with shoes
the absence of loot
spawns this absolute -
the poor are expected to lose

we have our very own damp course
now we grow mushrooms and mould
they won't let us move
so things can't improve -
the poor tend to do as they're told

gold leaf adorns some cathedrals
our Liam plays truant for days
he likes to draw
on the walls and the door -
the poor sketch in unruly ways

some things just go without saying
there's no boxing ring without ropes
above burnt-out cars
are comets and stars -
but the poor should never have hopes

Straw Hat Dreams

Inside I'm a true thoroughbred
I'm Desert Orchid and Black Bess
It's a mix-up that I'm saddled
as a donkey at Skegness.

I see myself majestic
a leaping Lipizzaner -
failing that, a Thelwell mess
coming fifth at a gymkhana.

I've got breeding, though it's random,
I'm exotic, and it shows,
I've got llama in my lineage
which explains my stubby nose.

I may never be a winner
honoured in collecting rings
I'm quite glad that I'm a donkey -
donkeys carry kings.

Gone Away for a While

Part of me absconded
it wasn't planned
it happened.

Like a cockroach
I became used to
the darkness,

not preferring it
in any way,
not at all,

it's where I went
without planning
to go there.

Yet from the tar shadows
I could still
hear you,

wading through russet deserts,
a brilliant mirage
too far off to be defined,

always looking for
the laden, and
opening tombs.

It was your breathing,
cautioning:
'scuttling is pointless'
that coaxed me,

there being
no more
corners left.

CENOTAPH
'Whatever stains us, we rub into ourselves'   *Seamus Heaney*

The weight of war
the ire of rain
what crushed before
will lash again.

From longbow
to the sonic boom
who makes these plans
then leaves the room?

This quiet before
the straining storm
the ploughshare's back
in uniform.

We're ruled by fey
discordant kings
tanks pirouette -
still, the snowdrop sings.

Eating with God
(In stages)

Where unicorns, magenta beasts
and flocks of planets roam,
where miracles are needless,
thrives our translucent home.

The cross there is a table
of unsurpassed design
displaying bread of sorrow
and abnegated wine.

This all-sufficient banquet
this feast that does not cease,
prepared and served and hosted by
the war-torn Prince of Peace.

Family Stories

My mother fell off a veranda,
my brother became a gnu,
my sister, poor lass, was
chewed by an ass,
forgive me -
all this is untrue.

My uncle was butler to Stalin,
I've a cottage within Xanadu;
my father was sent
into Belsen -
that last line is terribly true.

Chase

The rippled glitter of the waves
below the sea, labyrinthic caves.
The thunderstorm
that booms, then fades -
this raucous God has subtle shades.

The candy floss of baby's hair,
the terror of the tiger's stare,
our private acts which bring disgrace,
the anguish on Jehovah's face.

The jamboree of all Creation
mirroring Divine elation.

The unseen pain
of God's complexion,
the silence of
the Resurrection.

All Things New

Glasgow's got The Gorbals,
Wales has got Port Talbot,
Dublin boasts O'Connell Street
So? We've got a dock called Albert.

It's great that we should celebrate
a waxed-moustache, quaint name
just think if Queen Victoria
had met a Prince called Wayne.

This place of living paintings
this breathing history book
once ran a nation's commerce
and then ran out of luck.

But these wharves
once banished to the past
have scaled decay's dark slope
these cast-iron hearts
now beat and greet
and generate new hope.

And now we dare to build,
and plan
rejuvenating schemes
a vision of what could be
a city of our dreams.

But the soul, not just the body,
requires stimulating growth -
a city's truly prosperous
when
it's renovating both.

Song of the Worm

Where I used to stay
was dark and treacle.
It was deep and fairly safe
but not that much happened there,
apart from the occasional shovel -
that was always upsetting.

Back then
I was very good at slithering,
past stones
between the roots of trees
along telephone cables.

I was also very good
at listening.
You may think that is strange,
as it is written
'worms do not have ears'.
But we do hear
and what I listened to was
the rain,
and bombs,
the troubled dawn,
and the song of the blackbird -
those notes that melt the morning.

That is why
I came to the surface,

and naturally,
although the blackbird
swallowed me,
that was not cruel.
What he did was
he took me into himself.
And now,
I am in a shining world,
it is no longer dark
or random
the shovel cannot sever me,
nor the landmine splay me.

And now,
each morning,
before the brilliant tones,
the blackbird asks me:
'Worm, what song would you
like to hear today?
For, it will be yours.'

All Things Pass

All things pass,
and all things pass -
Our balsa-wood kingdoms,
our down-sized armies,
our Telethons, the Pentagon.

Our West End Premieres,
our paparazzi frocks,
our Investment Certificates,
Fort Knox.

Our adamant opinions,
our examination grades,
our violence, our bombs,
our cross-border raids.

All things pass,
and all things pass -
Apart from Communion
and the Mass.

Sometimes Love

Sometimes love
loses itself,
becoming marooned
in our amnesia past,
although still sending messages to us
in broken morse-code
which say:
'Come and get me - I'm still here'.

Sometimes love
wanders around for years,
our missing Prodigal son and daughter
in gaunt suit and fragile gown.

And sometimes love
blazes back to restore us,
a weaponless cavalry
bugling joy and remorse,
as Paradise
carols its champagne sound
'that which was lost can be found'.

OF ALL ROSES

Of all roses,
with their music and subtle moods,
there is one whose stem sustains
an imperishable flower
all through the budding and becalming
of earth's capricious seasons.

Of all roses,
with their immeasurable memories
of battles and intimacies,
there is one whose thorns grow inward
so that when we hold it
we may be remembering a lost iridescence
where we soared and splashed and spun
a radix without curtains and corners -
all this before we began to bawl and bleed.

Of all roses,
whether in chuckling nursery or
slow march mausoleum,
there is still one which, when digested,
makes our lungs light again
and seeds a vintage harvest
in our fermenting souls.

In Celebration

KENWOOD CAPERS
(after W.H. Auden's *Nightmail*)

This is the plug for the Kitchen Mixer
that powers and propels
our Gourmet elixir;
there's sponges and home-bakes
with walnuts and prunes
and alien stews, and glazed macaroons.

There's Hot Pots with chump chops
and apricot jam, and unspeakable
savouries that come from a ram.
We've turnovers, tartlets
and tipsy-cakes -
life's catering managed
from births to wakes.

Puddings in the pantry
flapjacks in the nursery
made by penniless debs
on a fatherly bursary.
Giblet broth, game paté,
consommé with a bite.
Jilted spinsters in Chepstow
preparing Turkish Delight.

This is the Dough Hook,
Whisk and K-Beater,
industrious implements

turning treats sweeter.
No need to knead bread
such whole-meal jubilation
as we blend in the yeast
of emancipation.

THE MAMOD LITTLE DYNAMO

When all ago was what we were
whilst some played Snap,
and some Dan Dare,
some were Zorro, some loved Trigger,
but I adored a perfect figure.

Her waft could turn your nostrils numb
she slinked across linoleum
with chugging, percolated breaths
powered by the purple blood of meths.

How to define her drilled allure -
expansive, wheezing paramour.
Enduring, lubricated chassis,
my gloss, enamel Shirley Bassey.

She is my all, my mardi-gras
as tractor, wagon, vintage car.
A miniature to prize and coddle
(does not need batteries) - supermodel.

SITTING COMFORTABLY
(on G-Plan Furniture)

Slot 'F' into 'H'
slip 'C' into 'D'
the procedural patois
of prosperity.

Hang ballgowns and blazers
behind functional doors;
aspire and direct -
the kingdom is yours.

Take the brevity of Bauhaus
to the Crescents of Thames Ditton
and establish tidy lounges
for the betterment of Britain.

Build suburban Athenaeums
from Lancaster to Liss
let catalogues create
a realm of timbered bliss.

Let everything shine -
a gala of teak,
bees-waxed and buffed,
suave, smart and sleek.

And to further enrich domesticity
the next must-have ideal -
a conservatory.

UNDERNEATH THE ARCHES
(is the Wellington Boot)

From xenophobic battles
to thatched pubs in the shires,
from a pied-a-terre in Eaton Square
to dung-scented Scottish byres

egalitarian footwear trudges,
strides and synthesises -
the rose-bush-pruning Dowager,
with the farm hand from Devizes.

For the Wellington's impartial
as it squelches through the clay
worn by equine, jodhpured Marquesses
and grooms on lower pay.

And the Wellington is shelter,
it's also rather chic,
a stylish sanctum for the soul
when the weather's turning bleak.

For the Wellington's a sailor
a brine-sprayed rubber breed,
complete on North Sea trawlers
or casting on the Tweed.

For the Wellington is culinary -
if you're drunk and blootered tight
place prime beef in the left one
and braise it overnight.

And the Wellington is faithful
and the Wellington is sure
but never let your socks fall down
as they'll chafe your calves red raw.

KIT INSPECTION
(Airfix on parade)

Glue the gunnels
paint the funnels
bring cannonballs
from secret tunnels
man the crow's nest
note the tides at Harwich
fix landing lights
chart spying flights
anticipate loud
blitz-krieg nights
write letters home
inspect the undercarriage.

Beware lest you should inhalate
rich fumes of butyl acetate
as that could generate
a kind of mania.
To convalesce from such
duress
avoid the minute Captain's
Mess,
especially if that ship's
the *Lusitania*.

Build Messerschmidts
from surplus bits
and register

audacious hits
by Spitfires
supervised by Douglas Bader.
Defend our soil
with the *Ark Royal*
the *Golden Hind*
and vessels loyal
and devastate
the dastardly Armada.

Exquisite toy
that can annoy,
diminishing adhesive joy,
when wheels drop off
your fierce F1-11.
But persevere
in second gear
with picnic hamper,
maps, and steer
your Blower Bentley
on a jaunt to Devon.

The Ten of Hearts

No. 1	Exclusive
No. 2	Imitations
No. 3	Naming
No. 4	Festival
No. 5	Model
No. 6	Slay
No. 7	Betray
No. 8	Plunder
No. 9	Slander
No. 10	Envy

No. 1

I've seen them come,
I've watched them go.
Inevitably, there are more on the way.

Dictators, emperors, maniacs,
tyrants in formal suits,
camera adept scoundrels,
potentates, buffoons,
wizards, warlocks in uniforms,
elected sorcerers,
below-average mediums,
inaccurate prophets,
gurus, gargoyles,
presidents for life, adept philanderers,
self-appointed generals
with tidal-wave armies,
methodical torturers.

And then there were the more
personable ones
who promised you elusive trinkets,
treasure, pleasure,
portfolios of happiness.
It's no wonder I have My weary days.

I have catalogued all such claims,
brooded over myriad manifestos,
read reports,

repeated names to Myself,
wept and yawned.

How could you?
How could you have been so gullible?
You put your crosses, waved flags,
sent off your coupons,
worshipped,
became cynical and despondent,
to be replaced by the next generation.

And as for those, who with Me
laughed at the impertinence of it all,
and met terrible ends,
they are now
being suckled in paradise.
There are new arrivals every day.

What I have said I have said.
Love has its laws.
My patience over this
is not everlasting.
You have ceased to study
My bloodied heart.

No. 2

Adoration, veneration,
from such a holy place.
Difficult to keep pristine
but easy to deface.

Supplication, exaltation;
beguiled priorities,
your acts of consummation
with quicksand forgeries.

Imitation, simulation
and emulatory.
Though idols have their moments,
I Am Eternity.

What counterfeit can promise you
a new, unsullied start?
So yield to Me, My blemished love,
betroth your damaged heart.

No. 3

You say My Name every day.
I am so often on your lips
through your instant expletives
and casual curses.
I am the exclamation
of your urges, and despising,
your wonder, and despair.
I am the empty hosanna
for all your hours.

So why do you say My Name?
It is not as if you know Me.
Some of you even gossip
about how you are intimate with Me,
and claim My secret touch.
So why do you say My Name?
It is not as if you know Me.

As for your names,
they are finite.
Some are fashionable and romantic,
others are functional, quirky, plain.
Some of you have changed your names,
you are not comfortable with them,
you regard them with melancholy
and as never really yours anyway.
Some of you have borrowed names,
and over that I hear your unease.

Some of your names recall antecedents,
people who emigrated somewhere and
had settlements named after them -
your name now holding
a heritage of perished events.
See how much I know about your name?
There is so much in every name.

So let Me tell you a little about My Name.
Unlike most of you, I did not need a
ceremony to receive My Name
for it has always been.

My Name is collapsing stars,
and My Name is the stallion's eye
and My Name is the
first eyelash forming in the womb
and My Name is the chase of the cheetah
and the earth's scarlet core
and My Name is ridiculous beasts
and unorthodox flowers
and My Name is sweet savours
and pungent odours
and My Name is that
which is too far ahead of you
and My Name is rivers and gates
and My Name has consequences
and My Name is an infinite scroll

So I say again, why do you say My Name?
It is not as if you know Me.

No. 4

Though I created you to stop,
you have forgotten how to.
And, having devised
your own calendar
in which everything merges -
like oceans meeting, you are,
at present, afloat
and treading water constantly.

On the surface
nothing much is different,
the waves are unremarkable.
What you believe to be the
distant shoreline
is concealed by mist.
You say to yourself:
'As soon as the palm trees are in view
I will swim to the fertile coast'.

Yet below your cycling limbs,
opposing currents duel and clash,
and you have not detected this turmoil.
And the undertow is carrying you
but you have not noticed.

And, like the shark,
you will now have to
keep moving,

without rest.
You have no option -
the days you have invented
demand it.

But,
while you are moving,
the shoreline
will remain unseen.

No. 5

This is a template
this is an intention
this is think outside yourself
this is an ideal and a practice
this is an ordeal and a privilege
this is a discipline and enlightenment
this is sweet seasoning
this is bitter herbs
this is myriad complexities.

[As for you, My bruised, bewildered ones,
whose parents have tainted and
terrorised you - think not of them.
Dissolve into Me, revel in Me,
refuge in Me.
I Am your Father. I Am your Mother.
I will give you honour.
I will consider. I will rectify.]

This is delicate
this is exact
this is beneficial
this is symbolic and literal
this is priceless and ordinary
this is wearisome and heartening
this is profound
this is necessary
this will prevail.

No. 6

First the treaty
then the war
with perches
for the vulture's claw.

Legislation
put in place
thus producing
funeral lace.

Duplicitous
peak-time charms,
kissing babies
selling arms.

Passion, rage,
the fatal blow.
Hidden Semtex
quid pro quo.

And where to now
with your schemes?
Seditious visions
shameless dreams.

You burn the skies
though I'm still here,
and you ignore
what should be clear.

Do not murder,
do not sin.
Suspend hostilities
within.

No. 7

How great was our garden
how teeming its shoots
how blazing its blossom
how melting its fruits

How vivid its fauna
how subtle its shades
its mystery oceans
and bronze esplanades

How fertile its timbers
how placid its beasts
how gilded its stairways
how stately its feasts

How tender its mornings
how countless its moons
its marble escarpments
and jasmine lagoons

Its Eros aromas
its primula nights
its quarter-tone birdsong
its infinite heights

But love's wedding carriage
is now a bleak hearse -
Indifference is painful
betrayal's far worse.

My sacred beloved,
you left Me to grieve,
you're in bed with others,
Oh, Adam.　　Oh, Eve.

No. 8

Using reason,
(which, by the way,
is only on loan to you)
you conclude that it is likely
that you will filch, swindle, loot,
fraud, lift, maraud -
choose whichever slang or legal term
you deem appropriate.
Appropriate - that's another stolen word.

So, because of your tendency
to take things, possessions, tribal lands,
hotel towels, childhood, tigers' teeth,
reputations, and so on,
you have come up with all manner of
gadgets, systems, and initiatives.
Initiative - that's something else that
doesn't belong to you.

So, let me remind you of just some
of your achievements:
burglar alarms, barristers, wigs,
insurance premiums, deposit boxes,
Dobermans, handcuffs.
Battering rams, moats, boiling oil,
missiles, tracking systems,
notices forbidding more than
two children in the shop at any time.

Tabloid fury, counselling for victims,
border guards, resistance movements,
snipers, closed-circuit cameras,
staff searches, immobilisers,
borstals, and *Crimewatch*.
Entry phones, alibis,
combination locks, PIN numbers,
perspex till covers, customs posts,
and DNA.
That last item is not yours either,
but you behave
as though it belongs to you,
which, technically, is fraud.

In fact very little is yours,
if anything at all.

You say:
'Disobedience is profitable,
and deception is lucrative'.
You have accumulated much.
I hope that when, eventually,
committal proceedings commence,
you have an
exceptional counsel
for the defence.
You will need it.

No. 9

*The dictionary of Satan,
the pawing of his hoof,
on the horns of a dilemma,
the goring of the Truth.*

Don't think of it as falsehood
more like getting by,
in order to be honest
it's requisite to lie.

For candidness is messy
and honesty's naive,
sincerity will cost you,
it's fitting to deceive.

Before your resignation
your praises will be sung.
I'm not so much spin doctor -
more plastic surgeon of the tongue.

And treason has its martyrs
and perjury its saints,
I've renamed these commandments
Ten Miserly Complaints.

> *The dictionary of Satan,
> the pawing of his hoof,
> on the horns of a dilemma,
> the goring of the Truth.*

No. 10

The poverty of palaces
the opulence of less -
this, My shepherd's wisdom.
I watch you crave redress
with lotteries as elixirs
for life's exacting toll -
all this yearning - temporal -
your heart a begging bowl.

And you explain your passions
with a 'Qué sera, sera',
through shiny assignations
in your cob-webbed Mardi Gras.
But Shangri-La is shuttered;
Nirvana's dank with mould.
True treasures are conundrums,
like, shanty towns of gold.

The perfumes of Arabia,
the linens of the East.
My bequests that should
dumfound you,
I will lavish
on the least.

COMMON PRAYERS

How to Build a Sanctuary

How to build a sanctuary?
With fire doors and stellar fountains,
dormer windows, and a ski slope
beside Artex-splattered mountains.

How to build a sanctuary?
In technicoloured pastel,
where pensioners can join the crèche
then hog the Bouncy Castle.

How to build a sanctuary?
Fulfil the regulations
with an altar made of butterflies
where death meets celebration.

How to build a sanctuary?
Where lions lie down with lambs,
and buttresses can really fly -
off searching for the damned.

How to build a sanctuary?
Without regard to cost,
an overflowing temple
for the worthless and the lost.

How to build a sanctuary?
With brass-embroidered dome,
where the blind see birds of paradise
and the homeless find their home.

GOD BEYOND GOLD

God beyond gold
Who gives us our worth.
Lord Who is due
much more than praise.
King Who observes
from the deep night of space.

Release us from
the terrors
which haunt
and pillage our sleep.

Inhabit our dreams
with vivid visions
of Hereafter.

And may the uneasy waters
of our hearts
be walked upon
and stilled,
by the becalming Christ,
our Saviour in the dark.

Grieving

In the numbness and the shiver
of the aftermath
where memory
is our nurse and consolation;
unleash in us,
God of loss,
hearts that flood and drown
the hard glare of death.

In the chaos of the unexpected,
please show us
that You're there, God.

We need to hear Your memories -
like the walk
through Galilee's spring flowers;
and gaze on Your momentoes -
the nails someone
picked up afterwards.

Let us hear Your grief, O God,
as You now listen to ours,
and,
surround us
with Your great comfort.

Here's Hoping

Exuberant God
Who adores us,
Carefree Creator
of the far lands.

Fire us with the freedom
of Your blistering heart.
Detonate us
and make us dangerous for You,
unruly disciples
impatient with
the narrow and the drab.

Unreachable God,
breathing big
in undiscovered galaxies,
make us wild and tender for You,
eager with love,
here on
Your pearl earth.

LONDON MARATHON

From the discovery days
of our crayon years,
to the valiant paces
of our winter bones,
You are there, exceptional God,
cherishing our value.

From the brash sprint
of our invincible youth,
to the steady steps
of more measured times,
You applaud all our good intentions,
generous God.

And, in our concluding dash
down the ultimate straight,
may we see and hear
the risen, rosette Christ,
urging us on
to the welcoming line,
the festival finish.

By Special Request

(These you have loved)

I Believe

I believe in one God, the Father Almighty,
[although I have problems with
the word 'Father' - what happens if
he was violent, drunk, or just not there?]
Maker of Heaven and Earth
and of things visible and invisible
[which is a bit of a puzzle
because if something exists
but is invisible
how do you know when it isn't there?]
And in one Lord Jesus Christ -
[I believe Jesus was a great cook.
O to be given a fish prepared by Him!
I believe in imagination.
Imagine no imagination.
Hard to imagine.]
God of God, Light of Light,
by Whom all things were made
Who for us men, and for our salvation
[presumably that means women as well?
I believe in women.
So does the Church of Scotland,
but that's possibly to spite the
English General Synod.
The Anglicans two-thirds believe
in women - providing they can set up
a Working Party to discuss
having a conference, at the end of which

a Report is issued confirming the
matter is under consideration,
depending on the vote
seventeen years later.
Methodists and Baptists
acknowledge women,
but not so as you'd notice.
Brethren and Pentecostals
are constantly surprised to discover
that such an object as
a woman exists.
But Charismatics fully accept women -
providing they can edify the worship
with lots of swirly dancing,
and don't wobble
unnecessarily.
I believe that if I believed
in reincarnation I would come back
as anything but a woman -
a cowpat, or an escalator perhaps,
at least with both those categories
you don't stay trodden on for very long.
I believe in women
I believe in women
I believe in women
but leadership is male
leadership is stale
leadership is frail.
I believe leaders should be servants
and servants should be powerless.

I believe all leaders should spend
part of their training
playing on merry-go-rounds
and building sandcastles.
I believe the church should be a refuge,
a swing park, an embrace.
I believe that at the beginning of the next
International Healing Crusade
at some conference hall cathedral
the platform party should begin worship
by doing farmyard impressions,
followed by a competition to find
the best yodeller.
I believe in absurdity
such as kangaroos, cockatoos,
and saying the word 'bobble'.
I believe that people who, in deep sincerity,
go forward for healing
and do not experience it,
and are then told by the leader
it is because of their lack of faith
should then be able to belt that leader,
and then minister to him about his sin
of using emotional blackmail
as a means of control in public meetings.
I believe in the gifts of the Spirit -
bullying sick people isn't one of them.
I believe in the supernatural,
mysticism, and the raising of the dead;
it's just that there's not much call for it

at our mid-week prayer meeting.
I have problems with people who
proclaim that there's a man
at the back suffering with lumbago,
when, in fact, it's a woman
in the gallery, with cystitis.
It all seems so confusing,
so speculative.
For that reason I don't play
one-armed bandits either.
Not that I have
problems with gambling,
after all, what are investments
but balance-sheet bets, FT tick-tack?
The revenue from these little flutters
has kept some Christian organisations
going for years.
I believe Prosperity Teaching
is a rabbit's foot
being waved at the reality of poverty.
I believe we need a theology of money.
I believe in confession -
not positive, or negative -
just confession.
I believe in what my friend Martin said:
'drama is a tool, but theatre is art'.
I believe propaganda is
ideological Valium.
Propagandists are mynah birds,
excellent mimics,

but don't expect them to say
anything original.
I believe in doubt.
I believe doubt is a process of saying:
'Excuse me, I have a question'.
Propagandists hate questions
and, in so doing, detest art.
I believe in art.
I acknowledge one baptism
for the remission of sins.
I believe we should seek
the lost, unhealed child
in all of us,
cradle it, and say:
'you really are forgiven'.]

And I look for the resurrection of the dead.
[No more hearses,
or death's graveside curses,]
and the life of the world to come.

I believe.
[I believe in quite a lot.]

I'M DOUSING MYSELF

I'm dousing myself with cosmetics
to stop me from smelling quite strong.
Max Factor, Gillette,
I've tried them all, yet,
I'm convinced that something is wrong.

I go into Boots every Wednesday,
the assistants are ever so nice,
and there I buy Brut
to make me feel cute,
and soap that helps to kill lice.

Yet still I can smell this foul odour
that somehow I cannot explain.
I've even tried Vim,
my future looks dim,
'cos now I just foam when it rains.

So dear Estée Lauder do tell me
when my body is clean and hair dyed,
it must be a phase,
please help me erase
the sweat stain that lies
deep inside.

WORD PERFECT

If God had a felt-tip pen,
or perhaps a can of aerosol spray,
what would He write,
and where would He write it?

Would He be quirky,
like Michelangelo,
arousing curiosity
through ornate scribble
on the ceiling,
causing peering pilgrims
to stand on their seats?

What eternal ponderings
would be found up there,
amidst the hanging forests
of the spider's swaying kingdom,
and would it be written in Hebrew?

'Moses was born in Egypt
but Jonah comes from Wales.

Goliath was a giant flop.

Man love your brother,
but Cain wasn't Abel.

Houses cleared, then flattened -
we also provide a band,
'phone Joshua for details.

I needed a doctor,
so they send me Social Workers,
signed Job.

Judas didn't need the money.'

But then,
God's always written on ceilings -
the burning bugle called
Creation's First Light.
The beetle-black sky
at His Son's execution.
The celestial graffiti of a
star-scrambled night.

God's been expressing Himself
for Ages.

HIP-OP RAPPITY RAP

I'm sitting here on the 14th floor
in the limb replacement corridor,
my x-ray of some weeks before
confirms just why this leg's so sore,
and I've begged the femur specialist
to eradicate my starboard list.
I said: 'Please operate.
Make this pain desist'.
He said: 'Push off, son,
join the waiting list'.

He put me down, he put me down,
he put me down for a

Hip op rappity rap
I can't stand straight,
I'm a lop-sided chap.
Hip op rappity roo
my career is over as a kangaroo.
Hip op rappity squeaks
it's not much fun when your
pelvis creaks.
Hip op rappity ouch
only three more years of pain to go.

Well, they'd have to treat me quick
if I had something mean
like Egyptian typhoid

or a ruptured spleen,
but all I've got is a permanent lean,
I make Long John Silver
look like Torville and Dean.
They said: 'If you go private
there's a room for you,
with a colour television
and a tree-top view -
or why not do it yourself
at B and Q
with a saw, a ratchet,
and superglue?'

I couldn't pay, I couldn't pay,
I couldn't pay for a

Hip op rappity rap
I can't stand straight,
I'm a lop-sided chap.
Hip op rappity roo
my career is over as a kangaroo.
Hip op rappity squeaks
it's not much fun
when your pelvis creaks.
Hip op rappity ouch
only three more years of pain to go
only three more years of pain to go
only three more years of pain
only three more years of pain
only three more years of pain to go - Oh!

THIS DAY IN PARADISE

This day in Paradise
new feet are treading through
high halls of gold

This day in Paradise
new legs are striding over
jewelled fields in which
the diamond is considered ordinary

This day in Paradise
new eyes have glimpsed the deep fire
ready to flame the stale earth pure

This day in Paradise
new blood
the rose-red juice
that gushed at Golgotha
now ripples and races down the
pure veins of a recently arrived beloved

This day in Paradise
a new heart pounds in praise
a new body shaped by sacrifice

This day in Paradise
the daunting dart of death
has no point
no place, and no meaning

And
whilst we mourn and weep
through these human hours
this day in Paradise
the blazing embrace
between Saviour and child
goes on
and on
and on